SHHH...
DOWNLOAD
THE SECRET
BONUS PAGES

SCAN HERE

Hi, amazing you!

Growing up, I often struggled with shyness
and a lack of confidence. While I still experience
these feelings at times, I have learned some
amazing ways to shift my mindset and stay
positive and happy.

By using the simple games and activities in this
book, I have been able to let go of my fears and
look for thoughts that make me feel good.
I am excited to share these techniques with you.
I hope to provide a safe and encouraging space
where you can turn when you need a little pep talk
or help with how to make yourself feel better.

Here's the biggest thing I want you to know:
You are in charge of how you feel, and with
practice and perseverance, you can create so
many happy and exciting days for yourself.
I'm thrilled for you. Let's go!

with love, Jen

BELONGS TO

There are two ways to use this book.

1. This book is not meant to be read in order! Simply flip to any section, read the pep talk, try one of the suggested activities, then put it aside until you're ready for more. Keep this handy source of positivity and happiness at your fingertips.

2. If you're unsure of where to start, flip to a random page, and let the book choose a pep talk for you.

CHECK OUT WHAT'S INSIDE

BEING TRUE TO YOURSELF & HAVING FUN

YOU ARE A BIG DEAL

Hey there, amazing, kind, helpful, curious, and brave person! Just wanted to give you a quick reminder of all the awesomeness you bring to the world every single day.

Here's your reminder to celebrate all your little victories, like giving a presentation in front of your class or having the courage to raise your hand and share your answer, even if you're not sure it is right.

Your small acts of bravery deserve some major props, so give yourself a pat on the back (or a giant high-five) when you do something that takes courage.

Keep being amazing and don't forget to celebrate all your hard work and bravery.

ACTIVITIES

Reward yourself for your victories.

1. **Share your wins.** Tell a friend or family member about something brave you did today. Acknowledge your actions that took courage, even if they seem insignificant. Take turns. Ask your friends about their successes too.

2. **Did you accomplish something big today?** Take time to decompress. Snuggle in and watch your go-to TV or YouTube series, play a video game, listen to music, read, or draw. Reflect and be proud of what you did today.

3. **Start a victory journal.** Write down all the things you did today that made you proud. Whenever you need reminding of how amazing you are . . . go back and read everything you have accomplished.

You have to believe in yourself when no one else does—that makes you a winner right there.

— Venus Williams

Flip the page to write your list of victories.

YOUR
VICTORIES

*Write them down, draw them out, glue in pictures . . .
however you want to record your big and small victories,
put them here.*

BE DIFFERENT, BE YOU

You're a one-of-a-kind, super miracle! There are billions of people on this planet, but none of them are exactly like you. You are truly exceptional, and the world needs to see your amazingness in all its glory.

Go out there and embrace your uniqueness! Be imaginative, speak up, dress in your own style, and show the world your true colors. Don't worry about what others might think of you—just be the person you want to be. You are a spark of life, and you deserve to shine bright.

ACTIVITIES
Choose to be 100% yourself.

1. **Go thrifting.** See what funky finds you can dig up. Maybe it's a vintage shirt with a wild print or a pair of pants with some unexpected details. You never know who you might inspire with your bold fashion choices!

2. **Speak up.** It's totally okay to have your own opinion and speak up when you disagree with your friends. In fact, it's really important! So don't be afraid to speak up and share your thoughts, even if they're different from what everyone else is saying.

3. **Use your inner guidance.** By following your heart and your gut, you can make decisions that feel true to you and help you live your best life. Plus, it'll give you the confidence and direction you need to tackle whatever comes your way.

4. **Don't be afraid to be yourself.** Show the world who you really are. When you share your authentic self, you'll inspire others to do the same. Trust me, the world needs more people who are unapologetically themselves. Be 100% you!

I can't think of any better representation of beauty than someone who is unafraid to be themselves.

– Emma Stone

MOVE IT & GROOVE IT

Are you ready to kick your day into high gear and get energized? All it takes is a little movement and some good tunes. So, get out of bed or off that couch and start moving!

Regular physical activity is beneficial not only for your physical health but also for your mental well-being. Moving your body releases endorphins, which are known to improve mood and reduce stress. Find an activity you love that gets your body moving and feeling good. Whether it's dancing, jogging, or playing a sport, choose something that sounds like fun and try it.

Make movement a part of your daily routine, and you'll notice a positive difference in both your body and mood. Put on your headphones and get moving to your go-to playlist!

ACTIVITIES
Move your body.

1. **Move around.** Jump up and down thirty times while pumping your arms up in the air. Literally shake out any stress with this move.

2. **Find new ways to get active.** Try yoga, stretching, or roller skating. If you are moving your body in some way, you are good!

3. **Dance to your favorite music.** Turn your favorite song up loud as you get busy cleaning your room. Gather up those wrappers, hang up your clothes, and take the dishes to the kitchen. A clean room always feels more fun!

4. **Walk a dog or hike a new trail.** Fresh air and movement will get your endorphins flowing and lift your spirits. Pack snacks, of course!

5. **Listen to a podcast.** Put on an episode of your favorite podcast and take a walk until the podcast is over.

Flip the page for some more ideas on how to get moving.

30 WAYS TO GET
MOVING

1. Take a walk while listening to your favorite tunes.

2. Play catch with a friend.

3. How many times can you bounce a ball on your knee?

4. Flutter kick while lying on your back.

5. Hold a plank and do mountain climbers.

6. Do jumping jacks.

7. See if you can do a backbend.

8. Go for a run around the block.

9. Crab walk around the room.

10. Try a new dance move.

11. Try to jump and touch your ceiling.

12. Grab friends and plan a scavenger hunt.

13. Can you touch your toes?

14. Go to the park and swing on the swing set.

15. Play a game of Twister.

16. Jump rope in knee-high socks.

17. Take a dance class or join a dance group.

18. Hula Hoop in the back yard or at a park.

19. Have a living room dance party.

20. Go for a bike ride.

21. Play Frisbee with a friend.

22. Do a yoga video at home.

23. Walk or run with a friend.

24. Swim laps at a community pool.

25. Climb a steep hill or trail.

26. Organize a kick-ball tournament at a local park.

27. Take a group fitness class at your local gym.

28. Do a high-intensity interval training (HIIT) workout at home.

29. Play tag or capture the flag.

30. Go ice skating or roller skating.

Use the QR code to listen to the Get Movin'
Spotify playlist.

TURN ON THE SMILES

Did you know that the simple act of smiling can transform any dull day into a blast? That's right—smiling has magical powers that can boost your mood and make you feel happier. Plus, it's contagious. When you make someone smile, you'll end up smiling too. Sounds like a win-win situation to me!

Your mission today is to spread smiles wherever you go. Turn it into a game and see how many people you can make smile. Give yourself one point for each smile.

Have fun and spread joy. You never know—your smile might just be the pick-me-up someone needs today.

ACTIVITIES

Ways to make people smile.

1. **Greet everyone.** Take a walk and say "hi," wave, or smile at each person you walk past.

2. **Surprise a friend.** Grab a blanket, a bag of M&Ms and head to a park for a mini picnic. Lie on your backs and find shapes in the clouds.

3. **Spread inspiration.** Gather up several smooth rocks and paint inspirational sayings on them. Scatter them around your neighborhood for people to discover.

4. **Cheer someone up.** Send a friend a funny meme or make a funny face when you pass them in the hall. Go forth, brave smile warrior, and share the love!

Flip the page for a list of 40 texts that'll make your friends smile.

40 TEXTS THAT WILL MAKE YOUR FRIENDS

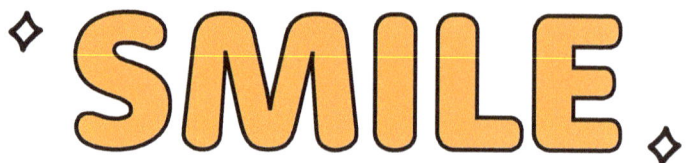

SMILE

1. I'm grateful to have you as my BFF!

2. You always know how to make me laugh.

3. I miss your face!

4. Hi, I just wanted to remind you how amazing you are!

5. Thinking of you today and sending lots of love your way.

6. You're the best BFF a person could ask for.

7. Thanks for always being there for me when I need you.

8. I appreciate your friendship more than you know.

9. Hope your day is going great!

10. I'm lucky to have you in my life.

11. You're the peanut butter to my jelly.

12. I love how we can always pick up right where we left off.

13. You always brighten up my day!

14. Thanks for being such an amazing listener.

15. I'm so grateful for all the memories we've made together.

16. You make my world a better place just by being in it.

17. Thanks for your support and encouragement.

18. You always know how to make me feel better.

19. I don't know what I'd do without you!

20. I'm so glad we met and became friends.

21. Thanks for always having my back.

22. I can't wait to hang out with you again!

23. I love your honesty.

24. I'm grateful for all our belly laughs.

25. Sending virtual hugs and high fives your way!

26. Thanks for always being up for an adventure!

27. I admire your strength and resilience.

28. I'm proud to call you my BFF!

29. I love how we can be ourselves around each other.

30. You're the macaroni to my cheese.

31. You always bring a smile to my face!

32. I'm grateful for our inside jokes.

33. You always know how to make my day!

34. I love your kindness and compassion.

35. I'm lucky to have you in my corner.

36. Sending positive vibes your way.

37. With you, I always feel I have a friend in my corner.

38. You're a rock star! Don't forget it.

39. You always know how to make me feel better.

40. I love your sense of humor. You make me laugh.

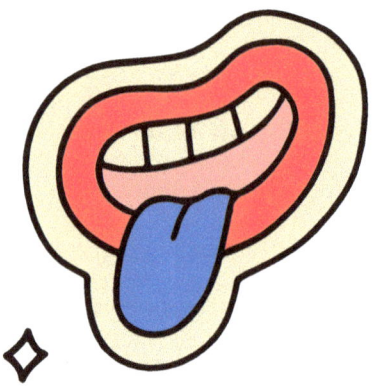

LAUGH IT OFF

Get ready to laugh. Laughing is always great, but especially when you are feeling grumpy or need some cheering up. A legendary comedian once said, "Laughter is the best medicine in the world." Go out and get your daily dose of funny. Whether you're naturally full of good humor or just in need of a good laugh, there are plenty of ways to laugh and boost your mood.

Laughter is a great stress reliever and is bound to make you feel better. Find ways to be silly, laugh and have fun.

ACTIVITIES
Use laughter to be silly and have fun.

1. **Play a game.** Gather friends and play a game like charades or Pictionary, where funny actions speak louder than words.

2. **Have a theme party!** Make it a high school prom theme or where everyone must dress up like movie characters!

3. **Fake laugh.** Make silly faces in the mirror. It will feel strange at first but keep going and you'll start to feel real laughter emerge. Do this with a friend for even more laughs.

4. **Try not to laugh challenge.** For a good chuckle, find a "Try Not To Laugh" video on YouTube and see how long you can make it without laughing. Good luck!

There's power in looking silly and not caring that you do.

– Amy Poehler

SAY YES TO ADVENTURE

Adventure time! If you're feeling down, stressed, or just plain bored, there's no better cure than creating adventures for yourself. Whether it's trying a new activity, exploring a new place, hanging out with friends and family, getting out of the house, or just experiencing something new, it is guaranteed to lift your spirits.

Mix up your same ol', same ol' routines and make adventures happen! You'll be so glad you did, and you'll have a blast while creating new memories with the people you love.

Who knows, you might even discover a new hobby or passion along the way. Get up, get out there, and have some fun!

ACTIVITIES
Ways to have an adventure.

1. **Do something out of the ordinary.** Try camping out in your back yard, exploring an antique store, or making s'mores in the microwave.

2. **Say yes.** If your friends or family ask you to join them in their adventures say yes. Especially if you have the tendency to say no.

3. **Create art.** Go to the dollar store and buy two canvases and art supplies. Grab a friend and both paint your own canvas for five minutes, then switch canvases and paint on the other person's canvas for another five minutes. Admire the masterpieces you created!

4. **Celebrate weird holidays.** Google weird holidays and celebrate them, like National Chocolate Ice Cream Day or Take a Bubble Bath Day.

5. **Document your adventures!** Take pictures so you'll have the little moments captured to remind you of all the fun things you have done. Scrap booking is a cool way to show off the adventures you've had.

Use the following pages to paste pictures and write about your adventures.

YOUR ADVENTURE
SCRAPBOOK

*Print your pictures, tape them down, and write about
the story behind each adventure.*

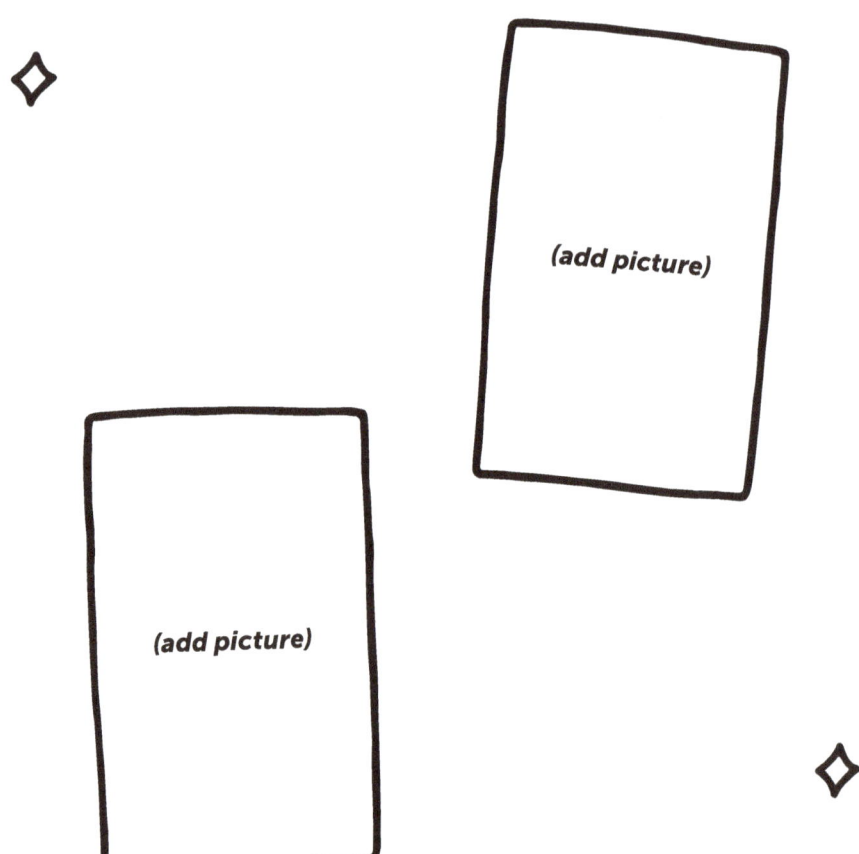

(add picture)

(add picture)

(add picture)

(add picture)

Draw doodles around each photo to add more to the story. Don't forget to date each picture too.

MAKE LISTS

Who doesn't love a good list? Making lists is a great way to focus your thoughts, organize your ideas, and compile fun things to do when you're feeling bored. Plus, they're an easy way to turn your yucky feelings around, helping you concentrate on the good stuff.

Next time you're feeling down or overwhelmed, instead of dwelling on what is going wrong, make a list of all the positive things that are going right. It'll do wonders for your mood and help you focus on the bright side of things.

Give list-making a try. It's a fun and useful way to help you focus on the things that you appreciate in life. If you are feeling good, and looking for fun, write a to-do list with all the exciting activities you'd be excited to try.

ACTIVITIES

Kick-start your list-making skills.

1. **Your favorite moments list.** In the morning, while lying in bed, think of three things that you are excited about for that day. For example, seeing a good friend or going out to dinner. Then, at night before falling asleep, think about the top three favorite moments from your day.

2. **Your favorite things list.** What are your favorite things to do? If it is watching movies, make a list of your favorite movies then rank them from 1 to 6. Roll the dice and watch the movie that corresponds with the number on your dice.

3. **Your library list.** Write down all the things you want to try such as drawing comics, photography, or cooking. Then go to the library and check out books on those subjects.

4. **Your appreciation list.** What do you appreciate? Write them down in your journal. Read through your appreciation list every time you need cheering up.

Use the following pages as a guide to help you write an appreciation list.

APPRECIATION
LIST PROMPTS

Answer the questions below to help remind you of all the things you appreciate in life.

What's the most important thing to you right now?

◆

Who are you thankful for and why?

What qualities do you appreciate about yourself?

What made you excited about today?

◆

What's your favorite way to make someone smile?

Write about an accomplishment you are proud of.

What are three good things that happened to you today?

What was the best gift you have ever received and why?

What are you most grateful for?

MAKING MISTAKES & BEING CREATIVE

NAVIGATING THE CREATIVE PROCESS

Remember when your art teacher would explain a project and show the class what the final piece should look like? Despite having the same instructions, you and your classmates all approached the project in unique ways.

Everyone has their own way of creating, and that doesn't make one approach better or worse than another. Instead, it means that everyone brings their own unique ideas and perspectives into their art. If you're working on a creative project and start to feel self-doubt, use this story as reassurance to keep going and see your project through to the end.

ACTIVITIES
Avoiding roadblocks
in your creativity.

1. **Don't know where to start?** Just make one mark on your paper, or write one idea to get the creativity flowing. Lower your expectations on how it should turn out, and soon, the next idea will come to you.

2. **Mid-project slump?** Now that you've made progress, you might think your idea, painting, or song is bad. Remember, you are still working through it, and bringing your unique perspective to the project. Don't judge yourself. Keep going.

3. **Don't want to finish?** If you are almost done and feel frustrated because it's not good enough, set it aside until you feel inspired to work on it again.

4. **Keep it for yourself.** You don't have to show it to anyone. Just keep it for yourself but keep going until it's done.

5. **Take your time.** You don't need to rush. Enjoy the process of creating and bringing your ideas into the world. Create things that make you happy!

You are capable of amazing things.

– JoJo Siwa

CATCH CREATIVE IDEAS

If you love to draw, write, or create new things, you know how necessary it is to have inspiration. But sometimes, inspiration doesn't come easily. That's where an idea notebook comes in handy!

An idea notebook is like a little treasure chest of creative ideas. Ideas waiting to be brought to life. Start by observing the things going on around you. Catch the ideas that jump out at you and jot them down in your notebook. Once you've collected your thoughts, you can use them to inspire new creative projects.

Challenge yourself to write down ideas in your notebook every day, and before you know it, you'll have pages filled with creative inspirations. Flip through your notebook whenever you need ideas for a painting, short story, science experiment, or game you're inventing.

ACTIVITIES
Start an idea notebook.

1. **Pay attention to pop culture.** As you read books, comics, magazines, or listen to songs, and watch TV shows, write down specific things you find interesting.

2. **Keep your eyes open.** What nuggets of inspiration can you find in your world that interest you? For example, look for new color combinations, textures, and shapes. Add those unique findings to your notebook.

3. **Keep your ears open.** When you catch part of an interesting conversation while waiting in line at school or at a store, write that story down in your notebook before you forget.

4. **Seek out diversity.** Go to cultural parades, festivals, and markets to find new inspiration. By embracing diversity, you can learn to appreciate different perspectives and ideas.

Turn the page and jot down your creative ideas.

YOUR IDEA
NOTEBOOK

*Ideas for creative projects can come from anywhere.
See something that sparks an idea? Write it down here.*

CREATIVE COPING

Being creative is a great way to cope with stress and anxiety. Drawing, painting, writing, or playing music relieves you from stress while giving you a sense of accomplishment.

When you are feeling stressed, make space for creativity. Dedicate time to being creative, whether it's a few minutes each day or for a longer amount of time on the weekends.

Adding creativity into your daily routine can lower stress and provide a positive outlet for self-expression.

ACTIVITIES

Use creativity to reduce stress.

1. **Find an art challenge.** Do an online search for doodle challenges or daily art prompts. These are a great way to inspire new creative ideas.

2. **Learn something new.** Attend an art workshop or watch an art class you find on YouTube to learn new skills and techniques.

3. **Take photos.** Photography captures the beauty in the world. Taking photos can bring a sense of calm and enjoyment to your day.

4. **Collage art.** Cutting and pasting images into a composition is a creative way to relax and unwind.

5. **Learn how to crochet.** Crocheting is meditative, plus, you'll make something that'll keep you warm. There are lots of videos online that will teach you how to crochet.

WRITE IT OUT

Writing will help you feel better by providing an outlet to release your emotions. When you write, you have the opportunity to process and express your feelings in a safe space. This is especially helpful when you are feeling overwhelmed or upset but not ready to talk about it.

Writing can also help you feel more connected to yourself. Whether you are journaling, writing poetry, or composing a song, writing is a powerful positive outlet for your mental and emotional well-being.

ACTIVITIES

Write to release your emotions.

1. **Put pen to paper.** If you were to write the plot of a movie, what would it be about? Try writing a song, short story, screenplay, or poem. Putting your emotions out on the page will make you feel better.

2. **You don't have to write alone.** Find a friend and write a story together. Each of you can write a part and then chat about what you like and what you want to change. Collaborating sparks creativity, and provides fresh perspectives and new ideas. Plus, it's fun to create something with a friend.

3. **Draw it out.** Once you have your story written, illustrate it as a zine (mini magazine) to bring it to life. If you want, share it with others.

Flip the page to learn how to create a zine that can showcase your story.

HOW TO MAKE A ZINE

1. Grab an 8.5" x 11" piece of paper (the kind you find in your printer)

2. Fold the paper in half

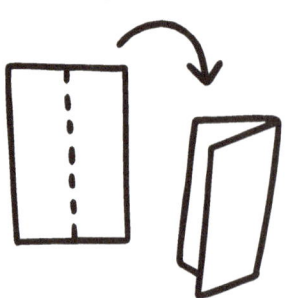

3. Unfold it, then fold the paper in half the opposite direction

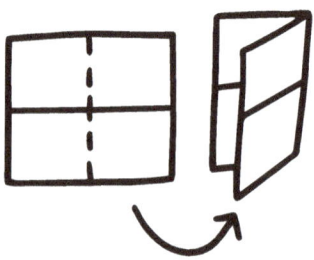

4. Unfold the paper so it's flat, then fold in both edges to the middle

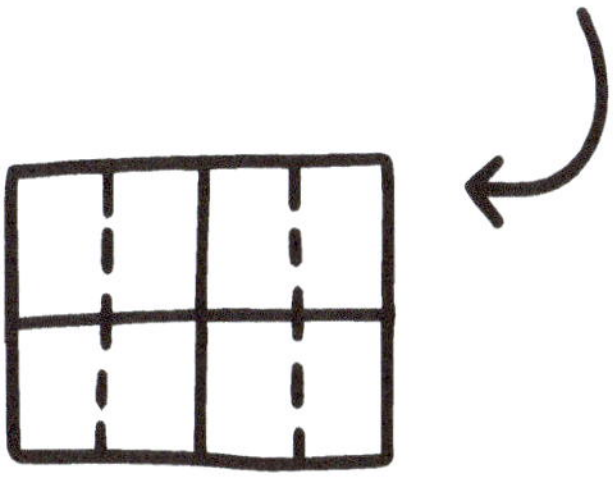

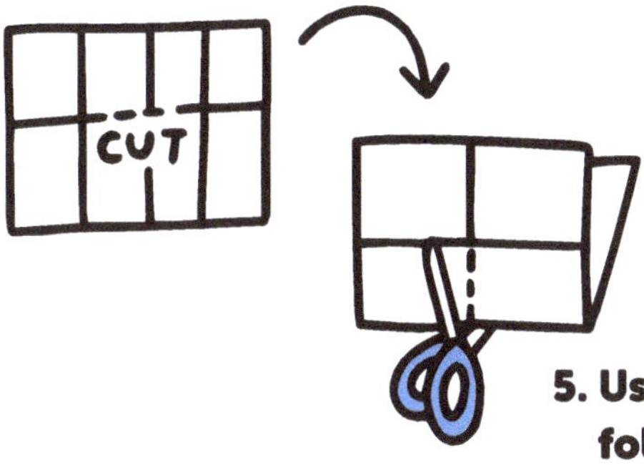

CUT

5. Use scissors to cut on the fold in the middle of the paper

6. Fold the paper inwards and press out the center cut to look like a plus sign and fold together to look like a book

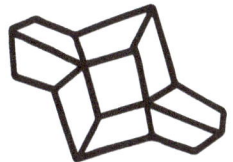

ZINE

7. Ta-da! Now you have a blank zine to start sharing your stories

MISTAKES ARE MAGIC

Today, imagine being on set of a movie! On this movie set, the director makes sure the actors are giving their best performance.

The director asks the actors to perform the scene over and over. Each time or "take" helps them improve and find new ways to say their lines.

Many times, the best "takes" come from happy accidents or mistakes made by the actors. That is what I want to suggest to you: Embrace your imperfections. Allow yourself to be okay with making mistakes. Keep trying new things and see what magic and inspiration comes your way.

Remember, it's all about the journey, not the result. Try not to judge yourself. Enjoy the process.

ACTIVITIES

Challenge yourself to make more mistakes.

1. **Try new activities.** Find something random to do, something out of the ordinary, something you know you won't be good at. That is the point of this challenge. Look for new activities to practice getting it wrong.

2. **Make the ordinary unordinary.** Bake a cake and frost it with your non-dominant hand. Have fun with the process, and don't take it too seriously because you still get to eat cake no matter how crazy it looks.

3. **Re-mix your talents.** What activities are good at? How can you do those activities in a new way? For example, if you like soccer, kick the ball using only your non-dominant foot.

4. **Set mini mistake goals.** Set a goal for how many times you can make a mistake during an activity you enjoy. For example, if you are on a sports team, set a goal to take a certain number of shots, even if you're not sure you'll make them. Remember, it's okay if you miss—the important thing is that you're trying and building up your resilience to feel okay when real mistakes happen.

Flip the page to check out more activities you can try to practice making mistakes.

PRACTICE MAKING
MISTAKES

1. Create an abstract painting using unconventional materials such as bubble wrap or a toothbrush.

2. Draw a portrait of a friend or family member from memory.

3. Create a sculpture using found objects, such as rocks, leaves and sticks.

4. Play a game of Boggle with a made-up language.

5. Write a song using random words from a dictionary or book.

6. Cook a meal using random ingredients.

7. Write a short story with a twist ending in just one hour.

8. Write a letter to your future self or a future generation.

9. Make a craft project using only recycled materials.

10. Create a poem or story in a different language using an online translation tool.

11. Learn to juggle or perform a magic trick.

12. Play a musical instrument with your eyes closed.

13. Learn a new dance.

14. Make a paper airplane and see how far it can fly.

15. Write a story or script using an online plot generator.

16. Draw a portrait of yourself as a cartoon character.

17. Create a stop-motion animation using everyday objects.

18. Make a piece of jewelry using unconventional materials such as paper clips or buttons.

19. Redesign a board game by inventing new rules and instructions.

20. Write a story or create a skit without using dialogue.

21. Create a 3D model of a building or structure using only paper, toothpicks, and glue.

22. Write a song or create a piece of music using only your voice and your body as percussion.

23. Make a painting using only one color and lighter and darker shades of that color.

24. Write a note to a friend using only emojis.

25. Build a Rube Goldberg machine using household items.

26. Make a video game with the online tool called Scratch.

27. Write a poem or story inspired by a random word generator.

28. Create a collage using magazine clippings or found objects.

29. Play a game of Pictionary or charades with random phrases generated by a website or app.

30. Play a video game on a difficult level, or try a game you've never played before, like chess.

NOBODY IS PERFECT

It's great to try your best and do great in school, sports, and art! But always feeling like you have to be perfect can make you worried and anxious. Remember, it's okay to give yourself time to feel carefree!

Personally, I find that the more I allow myself to be imperfect with my art, the more creative inspiration comes my way. Perfection is boring and, let's face it, impossible. Nobody is perfect, so it's important to be okay with imperfection.

Find times to let go of needing to be perfect. You will have so much more fun when you're not worried about messing up!

ACTIVITIES
Practice being imperfect.

1. **Messy makeovers.** Grab a friend. One person will be the "makeup artist" and the other will be the "face model." If you are the makeup artist, put a blindfold on yourself and create a makeup look on your friend. This is guaranteed to give you a good laugh! Then switch and have your friend do your makeup while blindfolded. Take photos of your new looks and tape them into your adventure scrapbook on page 28.

2. **Painting with your feet:** Find a large canvas or sheet of paper. Paint a piece of art using only your feet.

3. **Organize your messy room in a fun way.** Instead of stressing about making it perfect, embrace the mess and find creative solutions to organize your mess in a unique way.

4. **Messy obstacle courses.** Set up an obstacle course in a designated outdoor area. Engineer stations where you must use items like whipped cream, pudding, Jell-O, and water balloons in a challenging way before you advance to the next stage.

Flip the page for a drawing activity to practice not being perfect.

BLIND CONTOUR
DRAWING

Try this even if you aren't an artist. Draw an object or person
without lifting your pen or looking at your paper.
Enjoy being imperfect.

Only use a pen for this page. If you mess up, that's okay; let the mistakes shine through.

FINDING MOTIVATION & TRYING NEW THINGS

DISCOVER YOUR VALUES

It's time to let your voice be heard and share your ideas, values, and beliefs with the world. And what better way to do that than by writing a manifesto for yourself.

A manifesto is a list of beliefs that you create for yourself. It can be things you want to do, or ways you want to be. For example, you might create a manifesto that says you want to be kind to others, or that you want to try new things. Manifestos are a way to remind yourself of what's important to you and how you want to live your life.

Now is a perfect time for you to write a manifesto that reflects your unique personality and perspective. And remember, your ideas and values are worthy and deserve to be shared. When you feel confident in your beliefs, you'll be more comfortable sharing them with others. Don't be afraid to speak up and let your voice be heard.

ACTIVITIES
Write your manifesto.

1. **Write a list of values.** Think about what kind of person you are and who you want to be. Write down the values you feel are important in your life. Use short sentences beginning with the word "I." For example: "I am playful." "I am honest."

2. **Add personal stories.** Your own experiences can help illustrate your values and beliefs. For example, if one of your values is kindness, you could share a personal story about a time when someone showed you kindness or a time when you showed kindness to someone else.

3. **Add quotes:** Once you've figured out what's important to you, look for quotes from people you admire. You can then include those quotes in your manifesto to help express your own ideas and beliefs.

4. **Decorate your manifesto.** Use markers to add the finishing touches. Hang it where you can see it every day. Now you have a manifesto that is all about you and will inspire you to share your unique voice. Great job!

Flip the page to start writing your manifesto and discover what you value most.

YOUR
MANIFESTO

Take a moment to answer the following questions.
Need help thinking of different values?
Flip the page to see a list.

What are your five core values?

Explain why your core values matter to you.

What is your biggest dream in life?

What are you most passionate about?

What brings you joy?

How do you want to help the world?

Using all the above info, write one or two sentences about yourself.

LIST OF CORE
VALUES

Acceptance	Cleverness	Discovery
Accomplishment	Commitment	Drive
Accountability	Common sense	Effectiveness
Accuracy	Compassion	Efficiency
Achievement	Concentration	Empathy
Adaptability	Confidence	Empowerment
Alertness	Connection	Endurance
Ambition	Consistency	Enthusiasm
Assertiveness	Contentment	Excellence
Attentiveness	Contribution	Fairness
Awareness	Control	Fearlessness
Balance	Courage	Focus
Beauty	Courtesy	Friendliness
Boldness	Creativity	Generosity
Bravery	Credibility	Genius
Brilliance	Curiosity	Giving
Calmness	Decisiveness	Goodness
Candor	Dedication	Grace
Carefulness	Dependability	Gratitude
Certainty	Determination	Greatness
Charity	Devotion	Growth
Cleanliness	Discipline	

Happiness	Meaning	Stability
Harmony	Moderation	Stewardship
Health	Motivation	Strength
Honesty	Open-mindedness	Structure
Honor	Optimism	Victory
Hope	Originality	Support
Humility	Passion	Sustainability
Imagination	Patience	Talent
Independence	Peace	Teamwork
Individuality	Performance	Thankfulness
Innovation	Persistence	Thoughtfulness
Insight	Playfulness	Tranquility
Inspiration	Productivity	Trust
Integrity	Professionalism	Understanding
Intelligence	Purposefulness	Uniqueness
Intenseness	Reflection	Wealth
Intuition	Respect	Welcome
Affection	Responsibility	Victory
Justice	Restraint	Wisdom
Kindness	Self-sufficiency	Wittiness
Knowledge	Selflessness	Wonder
Leadership	Sensitiveness	Work ethic
Learning	Servitude	Youthfulness
Logic	Sincerity	
Loyalty	Spirit	
Maturity	Spontaneity	

CHANGE IT UP

Breaking old routines and creating new ones is like playing a game of UNO. When bad choices start to backfire, use a "reverse card" to help you turn a poor routine into a more productive one. It takes time and effort to create new habits, but you can do it.

Remember, just like in UNO, you have the power to change the game and create a better outcome for yourself. If you stick with your new changes for about a month, you can build a new routine that will make you feel better.

ACTIVITIES

Break old routines and create new ones.

1. **Make a list of your daily activities.** Include both the routines that are working and those that are not. Afterwards, circle the activities that make you feel good. Great, keep doing these.

2. **What things don't make you feel good?** Take a look at what doesn't make you feel good. How can you reduce or eliminate the number of times you do that? For example, if you have the habit of drinking sugary drinks, try swapping some of them to water . . . water will always make you feel better.

3. **Keep it up!** Stick to your new routines for about a month. That's how long it takes to make a new habit stick. Keep going even if it's hard at first. After a while, it will become easier and feel more natural.

Flip to pages 96-97 to read about setting new goals and routines.

INVENT A NEW YOU

You are the creator of your own identity! You don't have to be the same person you were yesterday—you can always re-imagine who you are at any time. And don't worry! This doesn't mean there's anything wrong with the person you are right now.

You are amazing just as you are! But if you're feeling ready to become the next great version of yourself, go for it! It's so much fun and easier than you might think.

As you continue to grow and discover new things, it's normal to want to invent a new version of yourself. It's all part of the journey of self-discovery. It can be so exciting and rewarding. You have the power to be the person you want to be.

ACTIVITIES

Reinvent yourself and your life.

1. How can you do things differently?
Think about ways you can change things up throughout your day. Maybe you've always wished to do things in a new way . . . now's the time begin!

2. Mixing it up. Here are some ways to mix things up. Start making your bed in the morning. Fix your hair differently. Wear your clothes in new combinations.

3. Who is the new you? Make a list of new ways to do things as the new you. Does the new you spend time every day working on a project or practicing music or playing a sport or hiking outside?

4. Be the person you want to be.
Start acting like the new you, and over time, you'll evolve into that person. You can be anyone you dream of becoming.

The key to my success has always been that my desire to succeed has always been greater than my fear.

- Dolly Parton

INVENT THE NEXT VERSION OF

*Answer the following questions to help develop
a new routine that is right for your needs and goals.*

How do you want to start
each day differently?

When do you want to wake up?
Will you make your bed?
How often will you shower?

What's one thing you want to
accomplish every day?

What are your favorite ways to move your body?

How will you spend your free time?

Who do you want to see or talk to every day?

What are you thankful for?

How do you want to end each day?

JUMP OVER THE FEAR

Trying something new can be scary, especially if you're not sure you'll be good at it. But that's okay because failure is just an opportunity for learning. In fact, the acronym FAIL stands for "First Attempts In Learning."

Think about how sad it would be if your favorite musician, athlete, or actor quit because they failed too many times. Even the great Simone Biles had to wipeout hundreds of times before she perfected her skills on the vault and balance beam. Even now, she's not always perfect, but she never gave up, and that's something she should be proud of.

The next time you want to try something new, don't let fear hold you back. Instead, set a goal, create a plan, and work towards it. And remember, it's okay to fail. It's all part of the learning process. With a little persistence and determination, you can accomplish anything you set your mind to.

ACTIVITIES
Keep a progress journal.

1. **Set a goal.** Write the goal you want to accomplish and the date by which you want to achieve it.

2. **Make a schedule.** Write down the dates and times you will practice. This is a great way to keep yourself on schedule. You'll be able to look back and see how much time you have dedicated to your goal.

3. **Take notes.** Next to each practice date and time, write about how you felt during the practice. Draw a happy or sad face so you can quickly see how you were feeling.

4. **Learning something new is hard.** You will try and fail and try again . . . and fail again! Keep going! You will improve, and you never know; you might just inspire someone else to keep working toward their goal too.

Flip the page to begin your progress journal.

YOUR PROGRESS
JOURNAL

Do you have something you've always dreamed of doing or achieving? Fill in your goal below and track your progress!

I, _____ **want to**
(insert name)

_____

_____
(insert goal you want to set)

because _____

_____
(insert why you want to set goal)

I hope to achieve this goal by:

_____
(insert end date to achieve goal)

x _____
(insert signature)

Date	Progress Report

Final Thoughts & Results

SAY YES TO SCARY

Are you ready to face your fears and try something that makes your heart race? Maybe you want to try skateboarding, singing a solo, or entering a slam poetry contest. If the thought of doing new things makes you feel nervous, that's totally normal.

We all get nervous when we try new things. So go ahead and give that scary thing a try. Remember to take a deep breath, be kind to yourself, and go for it!

Jen's Disclaimer: Don't say yes to peer pressure, things that will put your life in danger, get you into trouble, or make you feel uncomfortable.

ACTIVITIES

Grow your brave muscles.

1. **Stretch your courage.** Start small: Invite a classmate to hang out, or volunteer to answer a question in class. It takes bravery to go first, so raise your hand when the teacher asks for a volunteer.

2. **Get a little braver.** Soon, you will work up the courage to do something bigger, like enter a talent show or an art contest, or try out for the soccer or debate team.

3. **Step out of your comfort zone.** After a while, the things that made you feel nervous will now feel exciting. It might just become one of your favorite things to do.

4. **Keep track.** Make a list of all the times you've been brave in the past and write down how proud you felt for trying something new or facing a fear.

FOCUSING ON WHAT YOU WANT & ATTRACTING IT

IT'S YOUR SHOW

Are you ready to take center stage in your own reality show? "My Dream Life" is the perfect game to get you started on your journey to manifesting your best life.

In this game, you'll get to be the star, the director, and the script writer all rolled into one. You'll get to craft the plot, line up your cast (using your friends and family as inspiration), and you will bring the whole thing to life as the lead actor. It's an exciting way to visualize and plan out your ideal life.

But here's the thing: All the roles you play in this game are actually roles you play in real life too. You have the power to direct your life and set things up the way you want them to go simply by using the power of imagination and visualization. Give this game a try—you might just find that it's a fun, creative way to get inspired and start living your dream life!

ACTIVITIES
Visualize your day.

1. **Rise and shine.** Before you get out of bed in the morning, think about how your perfect day would go. Imagine, with vivid details, how everything will go smoothly for you.

2. **Flip the negative self-talk.** Nervous about something? Say encouraging things to yourself like, "I studied hard, I'm going to do well on the test today." "I'm going to have fun at practice tonight." Picture yourself having the perfect day.

3. **Nighttime recap.** Before bed, remember about all the good things that happened and everything you were grateful for today. Do this every day and you will be creating your best life. Because focusing on the way you want things to go, will attract more of the good things into your life.

4. **Host a "My Dream Life" party.** Invite your friends over to share their life visions. You can each plan what will happen in the next episodes of your shows. Using your imagination will help bring your dreams to reality.

PLANTING THE SEEDS

Are you ready to envision a joyful and fulfilling life for yourself? The first step is to let your imagination soar and dream up what you want your future to look like. It's like planting seeds for all the wonderful things you want to grow in your life.

One of the most creative ways to do this is with a vision board! To make a vision board, all you need to do is collect photos of the things you want and put them all together in one place. You can use magazine clippings, pictures from the internet, or even draw your own images.

Once you have your vision board all set up, make sure to look at it often so the things in your dreams stay strong in your mind. Start daydreaming about those ideas and goals coming true for you. With a little imagination and focus, anything is possible! Start planting those seeds and manifest the future you want.

ACTIVITIES
How to make a vision board.

1. **Visualize your dreams.** Think about what you want in life and what makes you happy. Imagine yourself living your dream life and achieving your goals.

2. **Collect materials.** Look for pictures of people you admire and who have achieved the things you want to achieve. Do you want to be a better gymnast? Cut out photos of your favorite Olympic gymnast. Also cut out inspiring phrases, or individual letters to create your own inspiring phrases.

3. **Create your board.** Use a large poster board or cork board as your canvas. Arrange the pictures and inspiring phrases on to your poster board. Remember to add your own drawings to make your vision board feel personal and help you visualize your goals.

4. **Display your board.** Use your vision board as a reminder of your dreams and goals, and take actions toward achieving them. Update your board as your dreams and goals evolve over time.

If you're positive and really excited and enthusiastic about what you're doing, it's going to happen, and it's going to happen big time.

– Shawn Mendes

Flip the page to begin your vision board.

YOUR VISION BOARD

Create your own vision board.
Glue or tape images of what you want in the space below.

YOUR MAGICAL JOURNAL

A journal can be a magical place where you write down your thoughts, dreams, and even solve problems. I know firsthand how helpful it can be to write down my thoughts and feelings.

Writing in your journal is an activity you can use to work through tough times or sort out your thoughts. Sometimes, it's hard to see solutions clearly until you write them down and look at them in a new light. Once you start writing, you'll have a clearer understanding of the answers inside of you.

Be open and listen to your internal guidance while you write. The goal is to explore different ways to solve your problem. Once you see the situation in a new light and you start to feel better, you'll know the right thing to do.

ACTIVITIES
Journal for answers.

1. **The writing warm up.** Start by writing the thoughts going through your head. It doesn't matter what you write at first, just start writing.

2. **Write down a question.** After you are warmed up, write a question you want answered. If you're having trouble with a friend, write, "How can I fix things with my friend?"

3. **Listen for inspiration.** Now, write thoughts and ideas that come into your mind about your question. Don't worry about what you write. Keep allowing your thoughts to flow through your pen onto the paper.

4. **Read it.** When it feels like all your thoughts are on the paper, you have come to a good stopping point. Go back and read what you wrote. Circle or underline the parts of your writing that give you the most hope.

5. **Focus on those good ideas.** Put your journal away and spend the rest of the day thinking about the possible solutions that have come out. Let this process help you feel better about whatever has been bothering you.

Flip the page for journaling prompts to help organize your thoughts on paper.

JOURNAL
PROMPTS

*Below are additional suggestions for topics
to write about in your journal.*

1. What is the most important thing to you?

2. What do you do when you feel overwhelmed?

3. You're proud of yourself because . . .

4. What qualities do you admire most about yourself?

5. Physically you are feeling . . .

6. Is there someone you want to forgive?

7. Why are you frustrated?

8. Secretly, you wish you could . . .

9. What fear do you want to overcome?

10. What would you like to learn? Why?

11. What are you thankful for?

12. What do you need to let go of?

13. What does success mean to you?

14. What do you need more of in your life?

15. What do you need less of in your life?

16. What is one thing you learned today?

17. Describe a recent challenge you faced and how you overcame it.

18. If you could have dinner with any historical figure, who would it be and why?

19. What does self-care mean to you? How do you practice it?

20. What is something you're passionate about and why?

21. What is one small thing you can do to make someone's day better?

22. Write a letter to your future self.

23. Describe your dream job and why you would love it.

24. If you could travel anywhere in the world, where would you go and why?

25. Write about a time when you felt truly happy and content.

26. What is one thing you're curious about and would like to learn more about?

27. Write about a moment in your life that changed you in some way.

28. If you could change one thing about yourself, what would it be and why?

29. Describe your perfect day.

30. What is something you've been wanting to try but haven't yet?

31. Describe a person who has had a positive impact on your life and why.

Flip the page to begin your magical journal.

YOUR MAGICAL
JOURNAL

Write down things that you have been dreaming about or what's been bothering you.

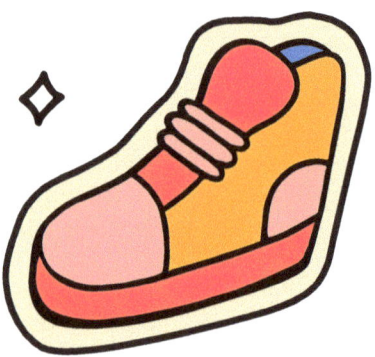

STEP INTO NEW SHOES

Are you struggling to make a difficult decision? Here's a cool game you can try: Put yourself in the shoes of someone you look up to!

The next time you are struggling to make a decision, step into the shoes of someone you admire and imagine what they would do if they were in your situation. This will help you see the situation from a new perspective.

Looking at your problem from a different angle, can help you find a solution that makes you feel better and a solution that is the right answer for you.

ACTIVITIES
How to see
a new perspective.

1. **Role play.** Imagine yourself in the shoes of someone you look up to. Doing this can help you find answers to your questions and gain new insights. The person you choose can be fictional, alive or dead. This person could be anyone from a grandparent to a musician you love. Choose someone who has the same outlook on life as you do.

2. **What would they do?** Imagine asking the person you admire what they would do if they were in your situation. Listen to the thoughts that come to you. Do any of them feel like a good solution? Use your intuition to guide you forward.

3. **Pros and cons.** Sometimes the answers come quickly. If your answer doesn't come to you immediately, make a list of pros and cons about the situation. This will help you see things more clearly and help discover the answer you're looking for.

ASK FOR HELP

If you feel you need some extra help with a problem, ask your spirit guides or angels for assistance. This is a powerful exercise that can help you tap into your spiritual support system. Your guides and angels are always there for you, ready to help you whenever you need it. All you have to do is ask for their guidance and trust that they will provide you with the support and wisdom you need.

I've asked my spirit guides for help with all sorts of things, like getting over the fear of public speaking, finding lost items, and finding the best parking spot!

You've got an infinite number of spirit guides. Ask them for help, and they'll be there for you.

ACTIVITIES

Get help from your spirit guides.

1. **Post a request.** Pretend you're posting a request on the spirit guide job board. There are athletic spirit guides, acting spirit guides, math spirit guides, art spirit guides, and so many more. Explain to them what you need help with.

2. **Be specific.** For example, if you feel nervous before your soccer game, you can ask your soccer spirit guides for specific help! You can ask them to keep you safe and guide you to be in the right spot at the right time. You can even ask them to help you play your best!

3. **Trust it's taken care of.** Now, have faith that your spirit guides will support you. Once the game is over, don't forget to express your gratitude for the help they provided.

4. **You can ask for help with anything.** Before bed is a great time to check in with your spirit guides. I love to ask mine to help me if I am having a tough time with a friend or co-worker. I'll ask my spirit guide to talk to my friend's spirit guide while I'm asleep. Together, I ask them to work out a solution to our problem by morning.

READY, SET, LEVEL UP

Are you ready to level up your art, music, sports, or studies? By mimicking the habits and practices of a successful role model, you can pave your own path to greatness.

Setting SMART goals is a great way to get what you truly want to achieve. SMART is an acronym for Specific, Measurable, Attainable, Relevant, and Timely. These five key aspects will guide you to where you want to be.

What goal do you want to accomplish? With a clear vision and dedication, you'll be well on your way to becoming the next best version of you.

ACTIVITIES
Find a role model to help you get to the next level.

1. **Choose your role model.** Find someone who is really good at the same sport, art, or hobby as you. This person will be your role model.

2. **Be a sleuth.** If you don't have direct access to your role model, find interviews or videos where they talk about their practice routines. How often do they practice? How long do they train each day? This will give you a better understanding of the commitment required to achieve success in your chosen field.

3. **Make a plan.** Use the routines from your role model to inspire your goals. Break down big goals into smaller, more manageable ones. For example, if your role model practices their sport for two hours a day, set a goal to practice for 30 minutes a day to start.

As you accomplish your smaller goals, you will build momentum and feel more confident in your abilities.

Flip the page to set a SMART goal.

TRACKING YOUR SMART GOALS

SPECIFIC

What do you want to accomplish? What skill do you want to learn? Define your goal and be as specific as possible.

MEASURABLE

Set specific milestones to measure your progress along the way. This will help you stay motivated and focused on your ultimate objective.

ATTAINABLE

Make sure your goal is realistic and achievable with the resources and time you have available. What specific actions can you set to help achieve your goal?

RELEVANT

Set a goal that truly means something to you. Ask yourself, why am I setting this goal and how will it help me in my life?

TIMELY

It's important to set an end date when declaring a goal. Decide when you'd like to have your goal completed and stick to it.

YOUR GOAL:

◆

---

*Write down each step of your SMART goal below,
along with start and end dates.*

S _____

M _____

A _____

R _____

T _____

Start Date: **End Date:**

FEELING ALONE, SELF-LOVE & FRIENDSHIPS

YOU'RE NOT ALONE

Feeling lonely is not fun, but there are lots of people in this world who can help you feel less alone. These people can be anyone from your neighbor or classmate to the bus driver or the person behind the counter at your favorite food spot.

If you're feeling lonely at school, try joining a club. It's a great way to make new connections and find people with common interests.

Doing something kind for someone can boost your mood and help you make new friends. Don't be afraid to talk to people and get to know them. You might be surprised how much you have in common. Making new friends can be scary, but it's worth it!

ACTIVITIES
Feel less lonely by focusing on others.

1. **Volunteer.** Volunteering is a great way to give back to your community and meet new people. You could serve food to people in need, or volunteer to help clean up after the animals at a local animal shelter.

2. **Reach out to new people.** A good way to make new friends is by saying something nice to someone each day. You could say something like, "Hey, I like your shoes!"

3. **It's not just you.** Don't be fooled into thinking you are the only one feeling alone. Everyone feels alone sometimes, even; the "popular kids" struggle with self-doubt.

Flip the page for phrases you can say to start up a new friendship.

PHRASES TO KICK-START A NEW
FRIENDSHIP

1. I'll wait for you.

2. You make me laugh.

3. Let's get food!

4. Wanna watch a movie?

5. How can I help?

6. Want me to go with you?

7. You'll do great!

8. This made me think of you.

9. Wanna go for a walk?

10. Let's play Minecraft!

11. Thank you!

12. Let's go shopping!

13. I saved a spot for you.

14. Come over!

15. Wish you were here.

16. Tell me more!

17. Let's bake cookies.

18. Wanna ride bikes?

19. I get you.

20. HUGS!

21. Come with us.

22. Good luck!

23. Text me when you get home.

24. I appreciate you!

25. You make me smile.

26. Movie marathon?

27. I'd rather hang out with you.

28. I miss you!

29. Let's hang.

30. I couldn't do it without you.

31. Let's go look at art.

32. You look great!

33. Let's have a spa day!

34. We're twinning!

35. Check out this TikTok.

36. I love your outfit.

37. I'll be right over.

38. Wanna FaceTime?

39. I have a surprise for you!

40. You got this!

41. Can't wait to see you.

42. Let's play mini-golf.

43. You're so talented!

44. You are the coolest.

45. I brought snacks!

46. Wanna get a smoothie?

47. I trust you.

48. You inspire me!

49. I'll go if you go.

50. Let's go bowling!

51. You're so funny!

52. I love your energy.

53. I'm so lucky to have met you.

54. I admire your creativity.

55. Thanks for being there for me.

56. You mean a lot to me.

57. Let's try a new hobby.

58. You make me feel better.

59. You're such a good listener.

60. I'm so glad we met.

61. Your opinion matters to me.

62. I love your style!

63. Let's plan a game night.

64. Let's plan a picnic.

65. I appreciate your honesty.

66. What are you doing Saturday?

67. You are amazing.

68. I'll lend you my book.

69. Let's go together.

70. Will you help me with . . . ?

FINDING YOUR TRIBE

Are you feeling a little down or disconnected? It's totally normal to feel that way sometimes, but don't worry. There are easy ways to boost your mood and feel more connected to the world around you.

Start by reaching out. Whether it's to a close friend, a family member, or even a supportive teacher or mentor. Surrounding yourself with people who care about you can make a difference in how you feel.

If you find yourself in need of support, reach out to someone you trust. Give them a call, send a text, or ask to spend time with them in person. You'll start feeling better soon!

ACTIVITIES

Create your support tribe.

1. Choose five people to be in your support tribe. It's important to choose people who you trust and feel comfortable confiding in. Your support tribe could include family members, friends, teachers, coaches, or camp leaders. It's important to have a mix of people who can offer different types of support and guidance.

2. Check in often. When you need a little extra support, a hug, advice, or just someone to share your feelings with, text or call one of the people from your support tribe. Let them know what you need. Don't wait until things feel really bad, connect with them often!

3. Find a mentor. Check out a mentorship program in your area. Many organizations offer structured programs where you can be matched with a mentor.

4. Reach out to a teacher, coach, counselor or even a professional therapist. They are trained to provide guidance and support you. They can offer advice and help you navigate challenges and find additional help if you need it.

Get support and encouragement from others as you work towards boosting your confidence and happiness. Join us on Geneva.

FINDING GOOD FRIENDS

Do you hang out with a small group of friends? Or do you have one large group? Maybe you have one or two special best friends you like to spend most of your time with. Or maybe it is a combination of all these.

Choosing your friend group is very important and can set the stage for smooth and enjoyable middle and high school years.

The most important thing when choosing friends is to feel good about yourself when you're with them. If you don't like how you feel around your friends, then I'd suggest looking for ways to make some new friendships.

ACTIVITIES
Find friends who are
there for you.

1. **Friends should cheer you on.** Choose friends who will be there for you when you need them. Good friends are there during both the good and bad times.

2. **Friends aren't mean.** Choose friends who don't make fun of you or gossip about you behind your back.

3. **Heart to heart.** You should be able to have conversations with friends without feeling ashamed, embarrassed, or judged.

4. **Phasing out bad friends.** If you have friends who make you feel bad, it's okay to step away from them. Be kind, but start spending more time with people who make you feel happy. It may be hard at first, but it will be better for you in the long run.

I define power by having the confidence to make your own decisions and not be swayed by other people.

– Adele

STOP COMPARING

Be mindful of how social media affects your self-esteem. Spending too much time on social media can make you feel bad about yourself, especially if you see pictures and posts that show unrealistic beauty standards, wealth, or lifestyles. Step away from social media when you start to feel down on yourself.

You are unique and have something special to offer. You have talents and strengths that make you stand out from the crowd. Don't let the fake facade of social media make you forget how amazing you truly are.

ACTIVITIES
Limit your time on social media.

1. **Take a break from social media.** It's important to limit your time on social media to maintain a healthy mindset.

2. **Set time limits.** Set a timer for twenty to thirty minutes. Once the timer goes off, it's time to put down the phone and do something else. This will help you avoid getting sucked into scrolling for hours. Now you have time to spend on other things that make you happy!

3. **Clean up your feed.** Unfollow people or accounts that make you feel bad about yourself. Make your social media be a source of inspiration rather than comparison.

I'm a big believer in accepting yourself and not really worrying about it.

– Jennifer Lawrence

EVERYONE GETS NERVOUS

Does the thought of going to a party or a new camp make you want to crawl under a rock and hide? Don't worry, you're not alone! Even the most social butterflies can feel anxious at times in new social situations.

It's normal to feel awkward and uncomfortable when you haven't been around a group of people in a while. Or if you don't know many of the people who will be there. Social situations can be intimidating, and it is okay to take a moment to collect yourself. Take some deep breaths if you feel overwhelmed. Be gentle on yourself.

ACTIVITIES
How to feel less awkward
at a gathering.

1. **Help out.** Ask the host of the party how you can help. Offer to help prepare the food or set the table. This will keep you busy until you feel more comfortable.

2. **Bring a friend.** Having a familiar face by your side can help ease social anxiety. Ask a friend to attend the gathering with you.

3. **Take breaks.** If you are feeling really awkward and need a break, head to the bathroom for a little alone time. Once inside, slowly take a calming, deep breath, hold it for five seconds, and exhale. Whisper to yourself in the mirror, "You can do this." Stay in there for a few minutes then head back out when you are ready.

4. **Be yourself.** Remember, everyone is unique. It's okay to be yourself. Embrace your quirks and let your authentic self shine.

DEALING WITH BULLIES

A bully will try to emotionally knock you down. Sometimes, that person may even be someone you consider a friend. They may write hurtful things on social media, spread rumors, or start a fight just to make themselves feel noticed.

A person who bullies others is covering up their own struggles and insecurities. Most of the time bullies are hurting inside and looking for ways to feel better about themselves. If someone is bullying you, it's important to remember that their behavior doesn't have anything to do with who you are as a person.

P.S. Think twice before you post or say something that might hurt someone else's feelings. You'll never know how much your words or actions might hurt someone else.

ACTIVITIES

Stay strong around mean people.

1. **Ignore the bully if possible.** If someone is being mean to you, do your best to ignore them and walk away. Bullies want to see if they're getting a reaction from you, so don't give them one.

2. **Distance yourself.** If a friend is being mean to you, it's okay to tell them you don't want to be treated that way. If they keep doing it, start to spend more time with the friends who are nice and do respect your boundaries. You deserve to be treated with respect and kindness, just like everyone else.

3. **Tell a trusted adult.** If the bullying is persistent or severe, it's important to tell a trusted adult. Whether it's you being bullied or it's happening to a friend, alerting an adult will start the conversations that need to be had in order to get the bully the help they need.

To learn about finding the right people to talk to about a bully, turn to pages 104-105.

DON'T GO TOO DEEP

Have you had a friend or parent get mad at you for something small or for seemingly no reason at all? When they snap or yell at you, it may not actually be about you, but about their own emotions and experiences.

Instead of getting upset, approach the situation with empathy and understanding. Ask them if everything is okay or if there's something bothering them that they'd like to talk about. This can help diffuse the tension and lead to a more productive conversation.

If that conversation is not possible, know you are resilient and have the power to ignore their anger. Focus on your own well-being and self-care.

ACTIVITIES
Distract yourself from their anger.

1. **Distract yourself.** Try not to take another's anger too personally, or let it sting too deeply. Don't re-play what happened over and over. Focus on something else like journaling, art, or deep breathing to help you feel better. The people you care about also have bad days, just like you.

2. **Let them cool off.** Hopefully, they will see that they overreacted and apologize. If they aren't the apologizing type, remember that they are human too, and they definitely don't have it all figured out. No one does.

3. **Try to move on.** It's important to forgive people and move on from past hurts. It doesn't mean forgetting what happened or just saying it was okay, but it means letting go of the bad feelings and not letting them control you. When you forgive, you can stop feeling angry and focus on positive things, like good relationships with others.

4. **Surround yourself with supportive people.** Don't hesitate to seek help from a trusted adult or professional if you need it. At the end of the day, your mental and emotional health should always come first. See page 143 if you need help.

BE YOUR OWN CHEERLEADER

Come on, let's give it up for the star of the show—YOU! That's right, give me a Y, give me an O, give me a U. What does that spell? YOU! You are totally worth cheering for. It's time to bring out your inner cheerleader.

Practice positive self-talk every day and build up that inner spirit. With a little encouragement from your biggest fan (that's you!), you'll have the skills and confidence to tackle anything that comes your way.

Give yourself a round of applause. GO YOU!

ACTIVITIES
Cheer for yourself.

1. **Write a cheer.** Every morning, say to yourself, "You got this!" Beginning your day on a positive note is the best way to start it.

2. **Recognize your own mean voice.** Practice being your own biggest fan by saying kind and encouraging things to yourself every day. That will help you feel more confident.

3. **State the opposite.** When you have thoughts that make you feel bad, like "My friends don't like me," it's important to remember that these yucky thoughts are like a warning signal from your soul telling you that something isn't right. To counteract these negative thoughts, you can call on your inner cheerleader to help you think positive thoughts instead. For example, instead of thinking that your friends don't like you, your cheerleader can remind you that you have great friends who love you.

If you have the ability to love, love yourself first.

– BTS

ROCKING A HAPPY MINDSET & FEELING GOOD

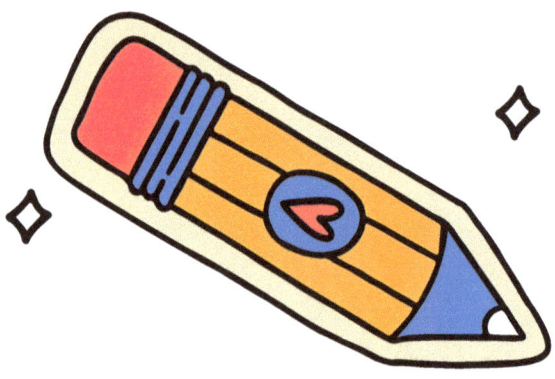

WRITE A NEW STORY

What stories do you tell yourself that hold you back? Are you stuck in negative patterns of thinking, convinced things won't go your way? Well, it's time for a plot twist!

Consider this: The majority of the negative stories you tell yourself are based in fear. Maybe something didn't go your way once or twice, but that doesn't mean it will happen that way for the rest of time. I hated roller coasters most my life because of one scary ride I took when I was a child. Fast forward to a family vacation at Universal Studios many years later, I decided to try a roller coaster and it turns out, it was fun! I am so happy to get rid of that old story.

Now is the time to ditch your old, limiting stories and write your new story. Imagine how much better you'd feel if you turned your fearful stories into new, more exciting ones.

ACTIVITIES
Feel good by rewriting old stories.

1. **What are your limiting stories?** It's important to identify your limiting stories and challenge them. Write down your top three limiting stories. Are they based in fact or fear? More often than not, the stories you tell yourself over and over again aren't true.

2. **Give your story a plot twist.** Flip those stories around. Write a new story that will make you feel better. For example, an old story could be, "I am shy." Instead, your new story could be, "Once I get to know people, I am relaxed and funny."

3. **Tell your new story.** Each time you think a limiting belief, recognize it and think of your new story. By replacing the negative story with a positive one, you create a happier and more powerful story for yourself.

It's a choice. You have to wake up every day and say 'There's no reason today can't be a the best day of my life'.

– Blake Lively

STICKY THOUGHTS

Have you ever stepped on a piece of gum, and it stuck to your shoe? Well, thoughts can be sticky too, kind of like that gum. They can get stuck in your head and it's hard to get rid of them. Just as gum collects dirt and grime as you walk, negative thoughts attract more negative thoughts.

If you're stuck thinking mad thoughts, it's going to be hard to feel better because more mad thoughts are joining the party.

Focus on hopeful thoughts and you will start to feel hopeful. It's that simple! That's why it's important to think positively and let go of negative thoughts that weigh you down.

ACTIVITIES
Choose thoughts
that feel better.

1. **Recognize when things don't feel right.** Identify what thoughts or situations may trigger your negative emotions. If you're feeling sad, angry, or anxious, do you know why you're feeling that way?

2. **Re-frame your thoughts.** What can you learn from the experience? Look at the situation from a different perspective. Try to see the silver lining.

3. **Shift your focus.** How do you want to feel? What can you do to change your thoughts or approach the situation in a more positive way? Keep in mind that it only takes 17 seconds of until more thoughts join in. Be mindful of your thoughts and focus on positive things.

STAND TALL, SUPER YOU

Are you feeling down? Are you anxious, afraid, or just feeling a little bit meh? Well, it might be time to check your body language!

Your posture has a huge influence on how you feel about yourself. Look in the mirror. How you're standing? Are you hunched over with your head down and shoulders scrunched forward? Do you shuffle your feet when you walk? Mumble when you talk?

There's a simple way to feel better: Power poses! Just by standing tall, with your head held high and shoulders back, you will give your brain a boost of confidence. You'll feel less sad and ready to take on any challenge that comes your way. Strike your best power pose.

ACTIVITIES
How to use your posture to gain self-confidence.

1. **Do a power pose.** Stand tall in front of a mirror with your feet wide apart, chest out, hands on your hips, chin up, and your eyes looking straight ahead like a superhero. Use this power pose to summon your confidence!

2. **Take up space.** When sitting at a table talking with a group of people, check your body language. Are you making yourself smaller by hunching over, crossing your arms and legs in tight? Sit up straight, uncross your limbs and take up a little more space.

3. **Make eye contact**: When you talk to someone, make sure to look them in the eye. This shows that you are engaged in the conversation and confident in yourself.

**Practice creates confidence.
Confidence empowers you.**

– Simone Biles

SKIP THE BAD SONGS

You have control over the music you listen to. You also have control over the thoughts you think. If you're in the habit of saying negative things about yourself, it's time to skip over those bad thoughts and choose thoughts that feel better.

Repeat good mantras to yourself. You'll find your self-image begin to improve. Scientists have proven this theory using plants. They yelled mean things to one plant, and it died. They said loving things to another plant, and it thrived.

Your thoughts are like the music you listen to, and you get to choose the tune that plays in your head. If you catch yourself thinking negative thoughts, try skipping over them and repeating positive affirmations instead. Just as plants thrive or wither based on the words spoken to them, you can improve your own self-image by choosing to speak kindly to yourself.

ACTIVITIES
Change your thoughts and you will feel better.

1. **What's on repeat in your head?** How often do you say, "I can't do that" or "I'm not going to try that, I'll embarrass myself?" Be mindful of your self-talk and try to replace negative thoughts with positive ones.

2. **Turn off repeat.** Repeating negative thoughts in your head is just like listening to a bad song on repeat. Hit the next or skip button to change the thought to an optimistic one like, "I may get it wrong, but it's okay, I'm still learning."

3. **Practice makes perfect.** When you start to feel worried, sad, or anxious . . . distract yourself and turn that thought off. This takes practice, so don't give up.

4. **Make a new playlist.** Create a new list of positive affirmations to help combat negative self-talk. Write them down and refer to them whenever you feel down on yourself.

Do whatever makes you happiest in this world.

– Harry Styles

IGNORE YOUR NEGATIVITY

We all have a little mean voice in our head. It tells us not to try new things when we are nervous, or it tell us to stay quiet because we might embarrass ourselves.

It's important to remember this negative voice isn't really you. Don't listen to it when it tries to make you feel bad about yourself.

When you feel like you're not good enough, or when negative thoughts fill your head, it's just your mean inner voice. Ignore it, and you can choose to think more positively.

ACTIVITIES
Shush your negative voice.

1. Recognize what your mean voice sounds like. Get familiar with the types of things it says.

2. Be the boss over your mean voice. Give it a name. When your mean voice starts talking to you, tell it to be quiet! "Thanks Bunk, but no thanks, that is not true. I am good enough."

3. Don't stay small. If the voice in your head is telling you mean things, ignore it! It's not telling you the truth. It wants you to stay small and not realize how strong you are.

4. Talk back. Another way to combat your negative inner voice is to respond with positive and uplifting messages. Remind yourself of your strengths, achievements, and the things you're grateful for. Surrounding yourself with positive influences can also help drown out the negative ones.

Never ever let somebody stop you or shame you from being yourself.

– Lizzo

TACKLE THE BAD DAYS

Learning something new can be a bumpy ride. There will be times when you feel like you're stumbling in the dark, unsure of what step to take next.

You'll definitely make mistakes along the way, and that's totally normal. If things were easy all the time, it wouldn't be as fun or rewarding when you accomplish them. Those bumps in the road are guideposts to help you learn and move forward.

Don't get discouraged! Keep pushing through those growing pains, and you'll be amazed at what you can accomplish.

ACTIVITIES
Look at obstacles from different perspectives.

1. **Take a break.** Sometimes when you're faced with an obstacle, taking a break can clear your mind. Take a few minutes or even a few days, then come back to the problem with a fresh perspective.

2. **Re-frame the problem.** Look at the obstacle in a different way. Ask yourself, "What's the opportunity here?" Or "What can I learn from this?"

3. **Focus on what you can control.** Instead of worrying about the things you can't control, focus on what you can do to make progress. Break the problem down into smaller, manageable steps, and work on them one at a time.

4. **Brainstorm.** Think of all the possible solutions to the problem, even if they seem silly or unrealistic. This will help you think outside the box and come up with new ideas.

5. **Get advice.** Don't be embarrassed to ask for help. Sometimes a fresh set of eyes can see opportunities you may have missed.

You're only human. You don't have to have it together every minute of the day.

– Anne Hathaway

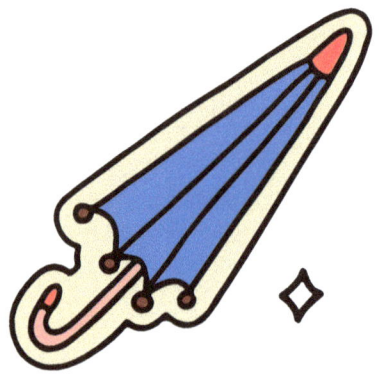

LET THE ANGER ROLL OFF

When you feel angry, your body becomes tense and your breathing and heart rate speed up. Using relaxation techniques can help release anger.

Think of breathing techniques as an umbrella that shields you from the rain of frustration. Controlling your breath can help you stay calm and make those angry feelings roll off you.

Taking quiet time for yourself and focusing on your breath is a helpful habit to develop. When you practice breathing calmly you'll release stress and anger before they have a chance to build up.

ACTIVITIES
Breathing techniques to help calm you down.

1. **Breathing.** Close your eyes and slowly inhale. Breathe in as you count to five. Hold the breath as you count to five again. Then count to ten as you exhale. Imagine any anger you are feeling is slowly rolling off your body. Repeat this exercise several times until you feel more in control.

2. **Golden light.** Visualize a warm, comforting light shining down from above, wrapping your entire body in a gentle, golden glow. Feel the peaceful and calming energy spread throughout your body, easing any tension or anger you are feeling.

3. **Take a shower.** As the hot water cascades over you, imagine it washing away your anger and frustrations. Allow yourself to fully relax. When you step out of the shower, you'll be able to move forward with a calmer mind.

4. **Squeeze and release.** Start with your jaw, hold it tight, and then relax it. Next, work your way down your body tensing and relaxing every part—your shoulders, your arms, your hands, your butt muscles, and your thighs. By the time you get to your toes, your body should be completely relaxed.

There are going to be bad days . . . but rainbows always come after the darkest storm.

– Demi Lavato

SAY NO TO FEAR

It's natural to feel afraid when facing something new or unknown, but it's important not to let fear hold you back. Fear prevents you from taking action and moving forward. Instead of getting caught up in the fear, focus on positive potential outcomes.

When my child was little, she used to be frightened by the loud sound of the school's fire alarm blaring during fire drills. Her anticipation of the alarm sounding made her so stressed and nervous that she didn't want to go to school.

We did the following steps together which helped her a lot. I suggest you try them when you have something that is making you fearful or anxious. They will help get the fear out of your mind, and you'll feel better afterwards.

ACTIVITIES
Send your fears far away.

1. **Imagine a ball filled with magical light.** Open it, put your anxious thoughts inside, and close it tight. Now your fear is inside this magical globe of light.

2. **Your fear is trapped.** Once you have placed your fear inside the magical ball, imagine it floating in front of you, as if it is trapped and unable to affect you. This way, you can visualize yourself separate from your fear and feel more in control of the situation.

3. **Close your eyes.** With your eyes closed take a few deep breaths and use your hands to slowly push the ball away from you. Watch it gradually float farther and farther away from you.

4. **Fear no more.** As you continue to watch your fear moving away, you will start to feel a sense of relief and lightness. The fear that once weighed you down is now getting smaller and smaller and will soon disappear into the vastness of space.

**It's not the absence of fear,
it's overcoming it. Sometimes you've
got to blast through and have faith.**

– Emma Watson

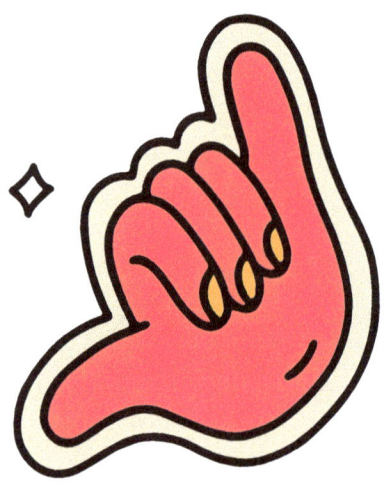

NO NEED TO WORRY

If you're a worrier, you're in good company. It seems like the human brain has been worrying about things since the dawn of time. But here's the good news: You don't have to waste your time and brain power on worry. There's a way to fix it!

Just like how you need to work out your muscles to make them stronger, you also need to practice making your brain stronger. If you practice thinking positively, you can reduce how much you worry. It takes effort and practice, but you can do it!

Start training your brain to stop worrying and watch it become more focused, calm, and in control of your thoughts. Don't let worry hold you back.

ACTIVITIES
Tell your brain to stop worrying so much.

1. **Ask why.** When you're worried about something, ask yourself, "Why am I worried?" Maybe you're worried about giving that speech . . . drill down further. Why is that? Keep asking why until you get to the root of your worry.

2. **Worry is annoying.** Think of your "worry" as annoying, imaginary friends. They try to make you nervous by talking about everything that could go wrong! You are the boss, not them! Tell them, "I've got this, be quiet!"

3. **What are you in control of?** Find a solution for each of the things you are worried about. For example, do you have a class presentation coming up? Practice giving your speech out loud until you know it really well. That'll help take away some of the worry.

4. **Think about it another way.** It's okay to worry about some things. That is only natural. But when you are really stressing about something, take a moment for yourself and re-frame it in your mind. By re-framing your thoughts, you may find that the situation doesn't seem as stressful or overwhelming as it did before.

TAKE AN INNER VACAY

We've all had those bad, awful days when it seems like everything has gone wrong and no one understands us. It can be really frustrating, and it's easy to take our anger out on others.

If you're having one of those bad days, step away from the situation for a bit and give yourself some time to cool off. Find a place to sit by yourself. Think about a happy place that brings you peace. Try a calming visualization to relax and reconnect with yourself.

ACTIVITIES

Visualize your happy place.

1. **Find a quiet, secluded spot.** Find a place where you can sit alone without interruption and where you feel safe.

2. **Close your eyes.** Take a deep breath and visualize a place where you feel relaxed. Are you at the beach or in the mountains?

3. **Sensory Awareness.** Do you smell seaweed, pinecones, or a bonfire? What sounds do you hear? Waves crashing, coyotes howling, or birds chirping?

4. **Imagine doing something active.** What are you doing? Swimming, hiking, building sandcastles, toasting marshmallows? Visualize the details and spend as much time there as you can.

5. **Return to your vacay spot.** Now that you have your special place, return to this spot as often as you need.

Flip the page for five steps to help with mindful meditation.

FIVE TIPS TO HELP WITH
MEDITATION

LOCATION IS KEY

Find a place where you feel comfortable. Grab a blanket or pillow to help you relax.

CHECK YOUR POSTURE

Find a comfortable place to sit but try not to slouch.

SET A TIMER

Before starting your meditation, set a timer for five or ten minutes. This will allow you to focus on your meditation rather than on the time.

EMPTY YOUR MIND

Focus your mind on a particular sound. Maybe it's your breath or the birds chirping, or the air conditioning.

TAKE DEEP BREATHS

Now that you are relaxed, begin taking deep breaths. Breathe in through your nose and out through your mouth.

A GUIDED MEDITATION

Find a quiet and comfortable place to sit. Close your eyes and take a deep breath in through your nose, and then slowly exhale through your mouth. Keep breathing like this, focusing on the sounds in the room, and feeling your breath rise and fall.

As you breathe, notice any thoughts or feelings that come up. Don't judge them, just observe them and let them pass like clouds in the sky. By observing them without judgment, you can develop a sense of detachment from them and prevent them from controlling your emotions and actions. Releasing your thoughts and feelings, allows you to feel more centered and grounded in the present moment.

When your meditation is over, take one more deep breath in and slowly exhale, bringing your attention back to the present moment. When you're ready, open your eyes and take a moment to notice how you feel.

YOU'RE NOT ALONE

I hope you've enjoyed this book. Life is about feeling good. You get to choose how you feel by the thoughts you think.

Do the activities in this book when you need some help feeling better. These are things you can do for the rest of your life. It takes practice so don't give up. I believe in you and want you to be happy.

I'd love to hear from you.
Email me at jen@skipthebadsongs.com.

much love, Jen

P.S.

Crisis Text Line
If you need help with eating disorders, self-harm, anxiety, depression, suicidal thoughts, or abuse, text the number below.

Free 24/7 Support.

UNITED STATES: Text HOME to 741741
CANADA: Text HOME to 741741
UNITED KINGDOM: Text HOME to 85258

National Suicide and Crisis Lifeline
Free 24/7 Support.
Call 988

HERE ARE SOME EXTRA JOUR-NAL PAGES 4 YOU

NEED SOME EXTRA SPACE?

You can use these blank pages to keep exploring your feelings, create art, or doodle to your heart's content.

ABOUT THE AUTHOR

Meet Jen Landis, she's an artist empowering youth to believe in themselves. She supports and uplifts youth through her company, Pincurl Girls.

Jen also founded the Art Gang, an online art club for girls ages 8-13. The club helps young artists gain confidence through art. Additionally, she hosts the GIRLBRAVE podcast where she interviews girls about how they exhibit bravery in their daily lives.

Jen can also be found teaching graphic design at the University of Nebraska, Lincoln. A former student, Rachel Dempsey, illustrated this book. See more of her work at DempseyStudios.com.

Be sure to check out PincurlGirls.com to learn more about Jen and see all the amazing work she's doing to empower and inspire tweens and teens.

ACKNOWLEDGMENTS

Thank you to Matthew, Sofia, and Stefan.
Your love and support mean so much to me.

Mom, you are my biggest source of inspiration!

Dad, you told me I can do anything and
I've always believed you!

A huge thanks to Margret Lukas, Cindy Conger,
Sara-Jane Schroeder and Rachel Dempsey
for all your help with this book.

This book printing was made possible, in part, with support from the University of Nebraska– Lincoln Hixson-Lied College of Fine and Performing Arts' Endowment Fund.

END NOTES

Do the superhero pose
This page is inspired by the social psychologist, bestselling author Amy Cuddy and her 2012 TED Talk, "Your Body Language May Shape Who You Are,"

Law of Attraction
This book is inspired by Esther, Jerry and Abraham Hick's Law of Attraction books.

Published by GIRLBRAVE Press

Copyright ©2023

Title: Skip the Bad Songs:
The Art of Rocking a Happy Mindset
by Jen Landis

Description: 1 Edition.

Subjects: LSH: Psychology of Self-Esteem
Psychology of Adolescents | Developmental Psychology
of Tweens and Teens

BISAC: PSY018000 PSYCHOLOGY /Developmental / Adolescent
SEL027000 SELF-HELP / Personal Growth / Self-Esteem

ISBN 979-8-9875331-0-9

Book and jacket design by Rachel Dempsey

Printed in China

THIS BOOK IS DEDICATED TO

SOFIA & STEFAN

**Always look for the happy path.
I love you!**